THE AMERICAN CIVIL WAR

CAUSES
OF THE
CIVIL WAR

A MyReportlinks.com Book

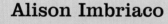

Alison Imbriaco

MyReportLinks.com Books
an imprint of
Enslow Publishers, Inc. **E**
Box 398, 40 Industrial Road
Berkeley Heights, NJ 07922
USA

MyReportLinks.com Books, an imprint of Enslow Publishers, Inc. MyReportLinks®
is a registered trademark of Enslow Publishers, Inc.

Library of Congress Cataloging-in-Publication Data

Imbriaco, Alison.
  Causes of the Civil War / Alison Imbriaco.
    p. cm. — (The American Civil War)
Summary: Reviews the causes of the Civil War, beginning with the
settlers who arrived in Jamestown, Virginia, in 1607 not planning to own
slaves, although thousands were already working in the New World.
Includes Internet links to Web sites related to the Civil War.
Includes bibliographical references and index.
  ISBN 0-7660-5186-2
  1. United States—History—Civil War, 1861–1865—Causes—Juvenile
literature. 2. Slavery—Southern States—History—Juvenile literature.
[1. United States—History—Civil War, 1861–1865—Causes. 2.
Slavery—History.] I. Title. II. Series: American Civil War (Berkeley
Heights, N.J.)
  E459.I45 2004
  973.7'11—dc22

                                    2003012112

Printed in the United States of America

10 9 8 7 6 5 4 3 2 1

To Our Readers:
Through the purchase of this book, you and your library gain access to the Report Links that specifically back
up this book.

The Publisher will provide access to the Report Links that back up this book and will keep these Report Links
up to date on **www.myreportlinks.com** for three years from the book's first publication date.

We have done our best to make sure all Internet addresses in this book were active and appropriate when we
went to press. However, the author and the Publisher have no control over, and assume no liability for, the
material available on those Internet sites or on other Web sites they may link to.

The usage of the MyReportLinks.com Books Web site is subject to the terms and conditions stated on the
Usage Policy Statement on **www.myreportlinks.com**.

A password may be required to access the Report Links that back up this book. The password is found on the
bottom of page 4 of this book.

Any comments or suggestions can be sent by e-mail to comments@myreportlinks.com or to the address on
the back cover.

Photo Credits: © 2003 www.clipart.com, p. 37; © Hemera Technologies, Inc., 1997–2001, p. 9;
Abraham Lincoln Historical Digitization Project, pp. 35, 38, 44; Library of Congress, pp. 1, 3, 11, 23,
27, 29, 31, 33, 40, 42, 43, 45; National Archives and Records Administration, p. 37; PBS, *Africans in
America*, pp. 16, 18, 21, 25; Smithsonian Institution, p. 13.

Cover Photos: All images, Library of Congress.

Cover Description: John Brown; campaign poster for

$200 Reward.

RANAWAY from the subscriber, on the night of Thursday, the 30th of Sepember.

FIVE NEGRO SLAVES,

To-wit : one Negro man, his wife, and three children.

The man is a black negro, full height, very erect, his face a little thin. He is about forty years of age, and calls himself *Washington Reed*, and is known by the name of Washington. He is probably well dressed, possibly takes with him an ivory headed cane, and is of good address. Several of his teeth are gone.

MyReportLinks.com Books
Great Books, Great Links, Great for Research!

The Report Links listed on the following four pages can save you hours of research time by **instantly** bringing you to the best Web sites relating to your report topic.

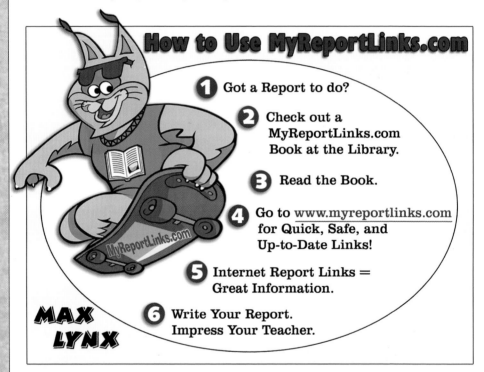

How to Use MyReportLinks.com

1 Got a Report to do?

2 Check out a MyReportLinks.com Book at the Library.

3 Read the Book.

4 Go to www.myreportlinks.com for Quick, Safe, and Up-to-Date Links!

5 Internet Report Links = Great Information.

6 Write Your Report. Impress Your Teacher.

MAX LYNX

The pre-evaluated Web sites are your links to source documents, photographs, illustrations, and maps. They also provide links to dozens—even hundreds—of Web sites about your report subject.

MyReportLinks.com Books and the MyReportLinks.com Web site save you time and make report writing easier than ever!

Please see "To Our Readers" on the copyright page for important information about this book, the MyReportLinks.com Web site, and the Report Links that back up this book. Please enter **WCW4762** if asked for a password.

Report Links

→ **The Internet sites described below can be accessed at
http://www.myreportlinks.com**

The American Civil War: The Causes
*EDITOR'S CHOICE

The American Civil War Web site provides a brief overview of the
causes of the Civil War as well as links to information about military
and political leaders, major battles, images, articles, and more.

►Civil War@Smithsonian
*EDITOR'S CHOICE

The Smithsonian Institution's National Portrait Gallery provides a visual
glimpse into the Civil War. This comprehensive site includes images of
soldiers, weapons, politicians, and life in general at the time of the Civil War.

►Fort Sumter: April 12–14, 1861
*EDITOR'S CHOICE

On April 12, 1861, Confederate forces fired the first shots of the Civil
War when they fired on the Union army stationed at Fort Sumter,
in Charleston Harbor. This site examines that battle.

►Africans in America
*EDITOR'S CHOICE

The PBS Web site *Africans in America* explores the history of Africans in
America from the earliest times, when they were transported aboard slave
ships, until the end of the Civil War, when slavery was finally abolished.

►Abraham Lincoln
*EDITOR'S CHOICE

At this Web site you will find a comprehensive biography of Abraham
Lincoln, the sixteenth president of the United States, who led the nation
during the Civil War.

►The Civil War
*EDITOR'S CHOICE

This Web site is a companion to the acclaimed PBS series on the Civil
War. It provides an in-depth look inside the battles, the people, and the
documents of the war as well as providing maps and other resources.

Report Links

The Internet sites described below can be accessed at http://www.myreportlinks.com

▶**African-American Mosaic: Abolition**

At African-American Mosaic, a Library of Congress Web site, you will learn about the abolitionist movement in America.

▶**African American Odyssey**

African American Odyssey, a Library of Congress Web site, explores the history of African Americans through images of both struggle and celebration.

▶**The American Presidency: James Buchanan**

This biography of James Buchanan, who preceded Abraham Lincoln as president, provide an in-depth look at the issues that shaped his presidency and his administration's policies that affected the nation. Secession began during Buchanan's administration.

▶**Causes of the Civil War**

At this Web site you will find a brief overview of some of the events and issues that, combined, led to the South's secession and the Civil War, including unfair taxation, states' rights, and slavery.

▶**Compromise of 1850**

American Treasures, a Library of Congress Web site, contains a facsimile of John Calhoun's speech (which he was too ill to deliver) during the debate which led to the Compromise of 1850.

▶**Confederate States of America Documents**

The Avalon Project at Yale Law School provides access to historical documents, including these related to the Confederate States of America. Here you will find declarations of secession as well as messages and other papers of the Confederacy.

▶**Crisis at Fort Sumter**

This Web site examines the events that led the nation closer to war after Abraham Lincoln became president, including the debate over slavery and the problems at Fort Sumter and Fort Pickens, in South Carolina.

▶**The Dred Scott Case**

At this Web site you will learn about the Dred Scott case, which in 1857 ruled that Dred Scott as a slave had no rights as a citizen and that slavery could not be banned in U.S. territories.

Any comments? Contact us: **comments@myreportlinks.com**

Report Links

The Internet sites described below can be accessed at
http://www.myreportlinks.com

▶The Eli Whitney Museum

At the Eli Whitney Museum Web site you can explore the history of the cotton
gin and learn about the life of Eli Whitney, its inventor.

▶A Fatal Contradiction

PBS's *Freedom: A History of Us* explores America's history from independence to
the present. In this episode, "A Fatal Contradiction," you will learn about slavery,
abolitionists, and how the inability to resolve the slavery issue led to the Civil War.

▶Getting the Message Out!

This Web site explores American presidential campaigns from 1840 to 1856.
Here you will learn how the issue of slavery and legislation including the
Compromise of 1850 and the Kansas-Nebraska Act affected these campaigns.

▶Harriet Beecher Stowe Center

At the Harriet Beecher Stowe Center Web site you can read about Beecher's life
and influential book, *Uncle Tom's Cabin.*

▶Henry Clay (1777–1852)

This site offers a biography of Henry Clay. Here you will learn about his early
life, his career in politics, the Compromise of 1850, and his death.

▶History of Jamestown

At this Web site you will find a brief history of Jamestown where you will learn
about the Virginia Company, settlers from London, and Captain John Smith.
You will also find a time line of events and a link to the National Geographic
Online exhibit of historic Jamestown.

▶John Brown's Holy War

This PBS site explores Brown's controversial fight against slavery. Here you will
find a time line of John Brown's life, a map showing where Brown traveled and
encountered other abolitionists, and brief profiles of people involved in his
crusade against slavery.

▶Jump Back In Time: Colonial America (1492–1763)

America's Story from America's Library, a Library of Congress Web site, tells the story
of Colonial America, where many believe the seeds of civil war were first sown.

Report Links

The Internet sites described below can be accessed at http://www.myreportlinks.com

▶**Kansas-Nebraska Act**

The Kansas-Nebraska Act of 1854 helped to strengthen the sectional divisions in the United States, which eventually led to the Civil War. At this site, you can read about the act and the effect it had on the people of the Kansas and Nebraska territories and throughout the country.

▶**National Underground Network to Freedom**

The National Underground Network to Freedom Web site explores the history of the Underground Railroad, which helped freedom seekers to escape slavery and find safe haven in the North and Canada.

▶**North American Slave Narratives**

The North American Slave Narratives Web site holds the text to a vast number of autobiographies and narratives of African-American slaves, recounting their lives before and after the Civil War.

▶**Northwest Ordinance**

At this PBS Web site you will find a brief description of the Northwest Ordinance, which prohibited slavery in the Northwest Territories—and eventually the states of Ohio, Indiana, Illinois, Michigan, Wisconsin, and Minnesota.

▶**The Papers of Jefferson Davis**

This comprehensive Web site provides access to a vast number of speeches and letters written by Jefferson Davis, the president of the Confederacy. You will also find a chronology of his life and a genealogy page.

▶**Statutes of the United States Concerning Slavery**

At the Avalon Project at Yale Law School Web site you will find many statutes concerning slavery in the United States, including the Fugitive Slave Act of 1850.

▶**Stephen A. Douglas Was Born April 23, 1813**

America's Story from America's Library, a Library of Congress Web site, tells the story of Stephen A. Douglas, Lincoln's opponent in the Illinois senatorial race of 1858 and one of his opponents in the presidential election of 1860.

▶**Today in History: John C. Calhoun**

Today in History, a Library of Congress Web site, provides a brief introduction to John C. Calhoun, who held the rank of congressman, senator, secretary of war and state, and vice president. Calhoun was a champion of states' rights and the institution of slavery.

Any comments? Contact us: **comments@myreportlinks.com**

Causes of the Civil War Facts

Time Line of Events Leading Up to the Civil War

1607—Colonists found Jamestown, Virginia.

1619—The first slaves are brought to Virginia.

1620—The Pilgrims land at Plymouth.

1688—Quakers demonstrate against slavery in Germantown, Pennsylvania.

1775–1783—The American Revolution is fought.

1787—The Northwest Ordinance is adopted.

1790—Samuel Slater brings the cotton-spinning machine to Rhode Island.

1793—Eli Whitney develops the cotton gin; Congress passes a stricter Fugitive Slave Act.

1803—The Louisiana Purchase adds more than 800,000 square miles to the country.

1816—Congress passes the first tariff to protect Northern manufacturers.

1820—Congress approves the Missouri Compromise.

1828—Congress passes the Tariff of 1828, called the Tariff of Abominations by Southerners.

1831—Nat Turner's band of slaves kills about sixty white people.

1832—South Carolina passes the Ordinance of Nullification and threatens to secede.

1848—As a result of the Mexican-American War, the United States acquires more than one million square miles of new territory.

1850—Congress approves the Compromise of 1850.

1852—*Uncle Tom's Cabin* is published.

1854—Congress passes the Kansas-Nebraska Act.

1856—Kansas elects two territorial legislatures, one proslavery and one antislavery.

1857—The Supreme Court decides the Dred Scott case, ruling that slaves have no rights as citizens.

1859—John Brown is captured at Harpers Ferry, Virginia.

1860—*Nov. 6:* Abraham Lincoln is elected president.

　　　　Dec. 20: South Carolina secedes from the Union, followed within months by Mississippi, Florida, Alabama, Georgia, Louisiana, and Texas, and finally by Virginia, Arkansas, North Carolina, and Tennessee.

1861—*Feb. 8:* The Confederate States of America is formed; the next day, Jefferson Davis is elected its president.

Chapter 1 ▶

The Civil War Begins

At 4:30 in the morning on April 12, 1861, Lieutenant Henry S. Farley fired the first shot of the Civil War from Fort Johnson in Charleston Harbor, South Carolina.[1] The cannon's mortar exploded over Fort Sumter, at the entrance to Charleston Harbor, with a resounding boom and a flash of light. It woke the people in nearby Charleston. People leaned from their windows, climbed to rooftops, or ran to the waterfront to watch the light bursting from guns. Many of them had been waiting for this first shot for months. They thought it was the beginning of something great, and they wanted to be part of it.[2]

Inside Fort Sumter, the men were already awake. An hour earlier, three officers from the new Provisional Army of the Confederate States had politely informed Major Robert Anderson, the U.S. Army commander at Fort Sumter, that the attack was about to begin.

In fact, during the months that Anderson and the men in South Carolina's militia prepared to bombard each other with cannons, they were polite about it. For example, as South Carolina's militiamen dug trenches and aimed cannons at Fort Sumter, one of the big guns occasionally went off by accident. Immediately a letter of apology would be sent to Fort Sumter. Once, as Anderson's men tested one of Fort Sumter's big guns, they accidentally fired on downtown Charleston, although the shot was not powerful enough to do any damage. Men quickly rowed

▲ The flag of the Confederacy flew above Fort Sumter on the day after the Union army evacuated the fort.

out to Fort Sumter to ask if Anderson really meant to start the war.[3]

Why would men who could be so polite to each other—men who shared the same values—be preparing to kill one another with cannons?

▷ A Question of Secession

Abraham Lincoln was elected president of the United States in November 1860. That election triggered the secession of South Carolina and eventually the standoff at Fort Sumter that led to the opening battle of the American Civil War. The people of South Carolina had decided that they could not be part of a country whose president would restrict their rights as a state and restrict

the spread of slavery. They believed that Lincoln's election meant an end to their way of life. On December 20, 1860, South Carolina officially seceded from, or ceased to be a part of, the Union, or the United States of America.

The Fight Over a Federal Fort

James Buchanan was the U.S. president at the time of South Carolina's secession. The days following Lincoln's election until Buchanan left office were the most difficult of Buchanan's term. Buchanan believed that South Carolina, and eventually the other Southern states that seceded, had no right under the Constitution to do so. But he feared that any action he took to punish the South would lead to war. So his policy was to let events take their course in the hope that the seceded states would fail to agree among themselves, and the Confederacy would break up.

On December 26, six days after South Carolina's secession, a U.S. Army garrison was moved from Fort Moultrie to Fort Sumter because the latter provided a stronger defensive position. Officials from South Carolina then traveled to Washington to demand that President Buchanan evacuate Fort Sumter and all federal forts in the state, which they no longer considered federal property since South Carolina was no longer part of the Union. Buchanan did not know what to do. Should he send supplies and more soldiers to Fort Sumter? That decision would probably lead to war. Should he command Major Anderson to withdraw his troops from Fort Sumter? That decision would admit that South Carolina had a right to secede, and Buchanan did not believe a state should be allowed to leave the Union. So he did nothing. South Carolina's governor, in the meantime, had the other forts

Tools   Search   Notes   Discuss   Go!

seized and decided to have guns trained on Fort Sumter so that it could not be fortified.

While President Buchanan did nothing about the situation in South Carolina, six other states—Florida, Alabama, Georgia, Mississippi, Louisiana, and Texas—also voted to secede. In February 1861, these six states formed the Confederate States of America and elected Jefferson Davis president. The new Confederate government then took over, and General P.G.T. Beauregard was given command over Charleston Harbor.

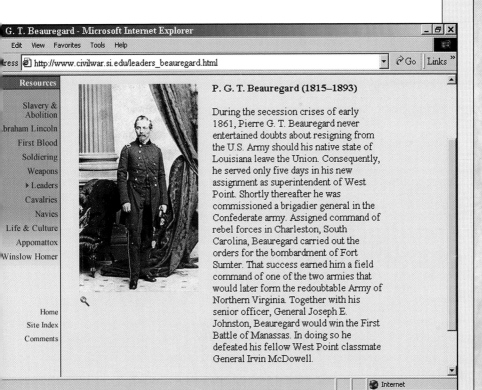

G. T. Beauregard - Microsoft Internet Explorer

Edit   View   Favorites   Tools   Help

Address http://www.civilwar.si.edu/leaders_beauregard.html   Go   Links

Resources

Slavery & Abolition
Abraham Lincoln
First Blood
Soldiering
Weapons
▶ Leaders
Cavalries
Navies
Life & Culture
Appomattox
Winslow Homer

Home
Site Index
Comments

P. G. T. Beauregard (1815–1893)

During the secession crises of early 1861, Pierre G. T. Beauregard never entertained doubts about resigning from the U.S. Army should his native state of Louisiana leave the Union. Consequently, he served only five days in his new assignment as superintendent of West Point. Shortly thereafter he was commissioned a brigadier general in the Confederate army. Assigned command of rebel forces in Charleston, South Carolina, Beauregard carried out the orders for the bombardment of Fort Sumter. That success earned him a field command of one of the two armies that would later form the redoubtable Army of Northern Virginia. Together with his senior officer, General Joseph E. Johnston, Beauregard would win the First Battle of Manassas. In doing so he defeated his fellow West Point classmate General Irvin McDowell.

Internet

Confederate general Pierre G. T. Beauregard, who ordered the first shots of the war to be fired, had briefly served as the superintendent of the United States Military Academy at West Point. He had held that post for only five days when his native state of Louisiana seceded from the Union, at which point he resigned from the U.S. Army.

On March 4, 1861, Abraham Lincoln was sworn in as the sixteenth president of the United States. A little more than a month later, Lincoln notified South Carolina that a naval expedition would be sent to Fort Sumter to fortify the U.S. Army troops stationed there who had less than six weeks' worth of food left. The Confederate government asked General Beauregard to deliver an ultimatum to Major Anderson: Leave Fort Sumter or be attacked. Anderson's reply—that his troops would evacuate the fort by April 15 unless he received other orders or his supplies arrived—did not satisfy the Confederates.

The Surrender of Fort Sumter

When the attack began on April 12, 1861, only 128 men were in Fort Sumter, and about 40 of them were civilians. They were surrounded by about seven thousand men.[4] For almost thirty hours, the battle raged. About four thousand cannon shells were fired, but not a single person on either side was killed during the battle.[5] Finally, when the fort was on fire and the food was almost gone, Anderson surrendered.

The Civil War had begun. The seven states of the new Confederacy had seceded from the United States of America, and were joined in secession by four more: Virginia, Arkansas, North Carolina, and Tennessee. The Union (the United States) believed that secession could not be allowed. What drove the Southern states to secede, though, was a long-running battle over their rights to control slavery versus the rights of the federal government to restrict or abolish it.

North and South: Two Cultures, 1607–1790

In 1607 a small band of English colonists founded the first permanent settlement in America at Jamestown, Virginia. They did not plan to own slaves, even though thousands of African slaves were already working in the New World. By then more than a hundred thousand African slaves worked on sugar plantations and in mines owned by Spanish and Portuguese colonists in the Caribbean islands and South America.[1]

The Jamestown colonists hoped to get rich by discovering gold as the Spanish had done in Mexico. They did not find gold, but they did find a climate that was good for growing crops, such as tobacco, that they could sell to England. In the Caribbean islands, Spanish and Portuguese plantation owners were getting rich; the English colonists thought they could do the same.

Virginia's First Slaves

Just twelve years after Jamestown was founded, a Dutch ship brought the first Africans to Virginia. Only twenty Africans arrived on that ship, and they were quickly put to work on the new tobacco plantations. Some historians say that these first Africans in America were indentured servants rather than slaves, meaning that they had hopes of fulfilling their obligations to their owners after a certain period of time and expected their children to be free citizens. Other historians argue that the English plantation

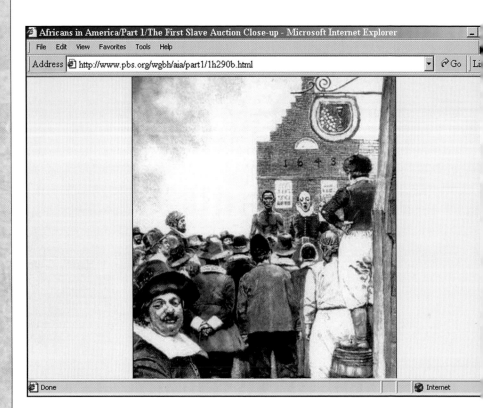

▲ *The buying and selling of Africans as slaves began early in colonial America. This twentieth-century painting depicts the first slave auction held in New Amsterdam (which would later be called New York City), in 1655.*

owners used the term "servant" rather than the term "slave," but that the first Africans in America were as much slaves as their children and grandchildren would be. In any case, it was a northern colony, Massachusetts, that became, in 1641, the first English colony in America to consider slavery a legal institution. And a Virginia court in 1663 ruled that the children born to slave mothers would themselves be considered slaves. The institution of slavery soon became embedded in colonial America.[2]

At first most of the Virginia farmers were not eager to own Africans. For one thing, the Englishmen did not trust people who were different, whether they were American Indians, who were also used as slaves, or Africans. Slaves were also expensive. But the settlers needed land that was cleared of trees and prepared for crops, and they needed to plant and care for their crops. There were just not enough English settlers to do all the work. Throughout much of the seventeenth century, most of that work was done by white indentured servants rather than African slaves.

Plantations—A Way of Life

Then, about 1670, Englishmen came from Barbados to what is now South Carolina. Barbados was one of the Caribbean islands where owners of sugar plantations were doing very well. But Barbados was crowded, so some of the planters came to South Carolina to start new plantations.[3] They brought their African slaves with them.

By 1727, about 78,000 African slaves worked in the colonies, many of them in the South, on large plantations. Less than thirty years later, the number of African slaves had increased to 263,000.[4] Plantations and the institution of slavery spread across the South.

The large plantations and the system of slave labor shaped the culture of the Southern colonies. The plantation owners had time for education, and they had money to buy things from England. Owners of the largest plantations became the leaders in their communities. People who came to the South without enough money to own a plantation often worked for the owners of large plantations and sometimes owned small farms. The poorer Southerners dreamed of owning their own plantations someday.

By the time the thirteen colonies fought for their independence, slavery was well established in both the North and the South. Not all African Americans were slaves, though. About five thousand free blacks fought in the American Revolution.[5]

▷ Life in the North

While colonists in the South learned to use slaves on plantations, the colonists in the North learned different skills. Although slavery was not as important to the way of life in the North, it did exist there.

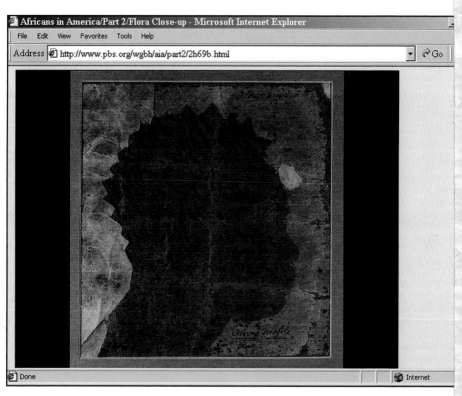

Africans in America/Part 2/Flora Close-up - Microsoft Internet Explorer

File   Edit   View   Favorites   Tools   Help

Address http://www.pbs.org/wgbh/aia/part2/2h69b.html   Go

Done   Internet

▲ *This silhouette of an African woman is believed to be that of a slave named Flora, who was sold to Asa Benjamin of Stratford, Connecticut, in 1796. This drawing accompanied the bill of sale. In 1784, Connecticut voted to gradually abolish slavery, but it was still a part of life in this northern state twelve years later.*

About thirteen years after the first colonists arrived in Virginia, the Pilgrims crossed the Atlantic Ocean not to find wealth but to find the freedom to worship as they chose. The Pilgrims and the other Puritan colonists who followed did not care that the climate in New England was not good for growing plantation crops. It was good for growing vegetables, fruit, and grains to make flour. The early New England colonists were willing to work hard on their farms. In fact, they believed that hard work was good for people.

▶ Northern Diversity

The New Englanders also wanted to be independent, and they made most of what they needed. By the time of the American Revolution, in 1775, the Northern colonies were making and selling all sorts of items, from hats and shoes to tools.[6] They built ships and sold them to England or used them for fishing. New England fishermen caught enough fish to sell to England too.

In 1682, William Penn, a Quaker, began another community based on religious freedom in what is now Pennsylvania. He encouraged Quakers and people of other religious backgrounds to come to Pennsylvania. When they came, these immigrants found an ideal setting for hardworking people with hardly any money to start their own farms and make good lives for themselves.[7]

The North did not have the rigid class system that developed in the South. In the North, a poor immigrant could work as a servant to earn money, buy some land, and, with some hard work, become a successful and respected person of the community. Unlike the Southerners who most often grew crops that they could sell to England, the independent-minded Northern

farmers raised crops that they could eat. They sold what was left over. Shipbuilders sold ships to England, fishermen sold fish overseas, and craftsman sold what they made in their communities.

Two Cities

A look at two cities, one in the South and one in the North, shows how different the two cultures were. Twenty years before the American Revolution, the city of Charleston, South Carolina, was spacious, tree-shaded, and elegant. Wealthy residents owned town mansions and rode through the quiet streets in fancy carriages. About eight thousand people lived in Charleston.

Philadelphia, on the other hand, was a bustling city where farmers brought fruits, vegetables, grains, and animals to sell. Hundreds of wagons arrived in Philadelphia's market regularly, making it a busy, noisy place. By 1760, more than twenty-three thousand people lived in Philadelphia. Sixteen years later, the population of that city was forty thousand.[8]

The American Revolution

The cultural and economic differences between the Northern and Southern colonies also figured in America's war for independence. Great Britain's strategy for victory was to separate New England from the rest of the colonies. It was thought that a victory over the Northeastern colonies would bring a swift end to the war because Britain believed that the large number of loyalists in the Southern colonies would cease to fight. Although that strategy did not work to separate the colonies, the divisions between North and South continued with the birth of the new nation.

North and South: One Country

When the thirteen colonies won their independence from Great Britain, however, the new nation had important decisions to make. One decision was what to do with the territory that lay west of the thirteen states. Settlers were already moving west into the Northwest Territory, which would later become the states of Ohio, Indiana, Illinois, Michigan, and Wisconsin.

Another important decision was what kind of government would make it possible for the thirteen states to work together as one country. Both decisions were made

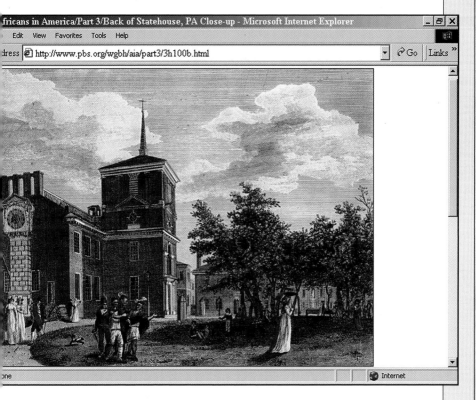

Africans in America/Part 3/Back of Statehouse, PA Close-up - Microsoft Internet Explorer

Edit   View   Favorites   Tools   Help

dress   http://www.pbs.org/wgbh/aia/part3/3h100b.html   Go   Links

Internet

▲ *Philadelphia in 1799. Northern cities like Philadelphia were growing rapidly as the nineteenth century dawned, while the South had relatively few large cities.*

in 1787, and both would greatly affect the future of slavery in the United States.

The Northwest Ordinance

At that time, there were people in the North and in the South who believed that slavery was wrong. As early as 1688, a group of Quakers in Pennsylvania demonstrated against slavery.[9] By 1780 the Underground Railroad, a network of people and safe houses, was beginning to help runaway slaves reach freedom in the North. In the South, some slave owners educated their slaves and helped them buy freedom. Others simply set their slaves free.

So, when the Continental Congress passed the Northwest Ordinance in 1787 to govern the new Northwest Territory, it included the provision that there would be no slavery in those western lands.

The Constitution

Later in 1787, delegates from the thirteen states met to design the U.S. Constitution, the set of laws that would govern the United States. The states had different interests and concerns, and the delegates realized that they would need to compromise—they would have to give up some things they wanted to get the things they wanted most. Two issues, especially, led to much debate and compromise. One issue was how states would be represented in the new government. Another was slavery.

The delegates compromised when they decided on two "houses" in Congress. Small states wanted equal representation when laws were made, while large states wanted representation according to their size. In the Senate, all states have two senators regardless of the state's population. In the House of Representatives, states are represented

▲ This painting of George Washington and his slaves presents an idealized version of the institution of slavery. Washington was not the only founding father to own slaves, nor were Southerners the only Americans to own slaves.

according to their population, although every state has at least one representative.

The decision to count slaves, who could not vote, as three fifths of a person was another compromise, as was the decision that the slave trade would not be made illegal until 1808. The delegates also included in the Constitution the statement that fugitive (runaway) slaves had to be returned to their owners.

Many of the constitutional delegates who made these compromises about slavery, including George Washington, who owned slaves, believed that slavery would gradually die out. But big changes were coming. Slavery was about to become more important than ever.

Chapter 3

Cotton, 1790–1818

As the American colonies were fighting to win their independence, the Industrial Revolution was just getting under way in England. New steam-driven machines changed the way that people made cotton cloth. Cotton cloth was comfortable to wear and easier to clean than other materials of that time. But it was very expensive to make—until the invention of the new machines. Soon England had factories, or textile mills, that used these new machines to make cotton yarn for cloth that people could afford. These new factories suddenly needed a lot more raw cotton.

An Englishman named Samuel Slater memorized the design for a cotton-spinning machine and brought it to New England in 1790. Soon New England states had cotton mills, too, and the demand for raw cotton increased.

Southern planters saw that there was money to be made in cotton, and the South was then the only part of the United States where cotton could be grown. But planting and picking cotton required many hours of hard work, so plantation owners needed more slaves. Removing the seeds from the cotton fiber so it would be ready for the cotton mills was slow, hard work too. A slave would work a whole day to clean just one pound of cotton.

In 1793, Eli Whitney, a Northerner, developed a cotton engine, or "gin," to separate the seeds from the cotton fiber. With Whitney's cotton gin, a slave could clean cotton fifty times faster than it could be cleaned by hand.[1] The cotton gin made growing cotton much more profitable.

Tools   Search   Notes   Discuss

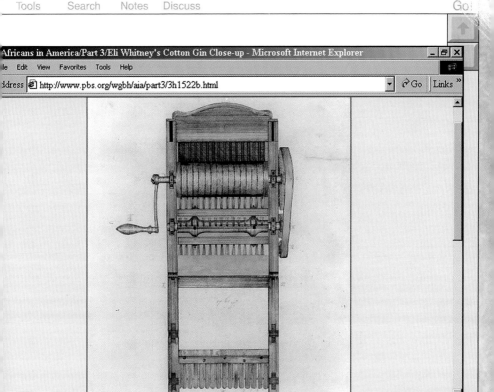

Africans in America/Part 3/Eli Whitney's Cotton Gin Close-up - Microsoft Internet Explorer

le Edit View Favorites Tools Help

Address http://www.pbs.org/wgbh/aia/part3/3h1522b.html   Go   Links

Done   Internet

▲ *The cotton gin made growing cotton more profitable and led to an increase in the number of slaves working in the cotton fields of the South.*

Cotton Is King

Within ten years, cotton became the main crop in the South. In 1790 before the invention of the cotton gin, about three thousand bales of cotton (a bale weighed between three hundred and five hundred pounds) were produced in the United States. About ten years later, almost one hundred thousand bales were produced.[2]

Cotton became "king" to the Southern cotton planters as they invested their money in more slaves and more land. As cotton became more important to the

South's economy, so did the slaves who worked on the plantations. Cotton brought millions of dollars to the South. From the beginning of the 1800s until the Civil War, cotton exports were worth more than all the other American exports combined.[3] By 1840, the United States produced more than 60 percent of the world's cotton.

Cotton in the North

Cotton brought great change to the North, too. Factories for making cotton yarn sprang up around New England. In 1814 a factory in Massachusetts brought together all the parts of spinning and weaving to make cotton cloth more efficiently. Soon Northern factories were making other things, too, from farming equipment to guns.

The factories provided jobs, and people came from Britain and Europe by the thousands to take those jobs. For example, between 1815 and 1820, approximately one hundred thousand immigrants arrived in America.[4] Most of them came to the North.

The North was changing. Most people were still farmers, but people could also find jobs in the factories and in the new towns and cities. The Northern population grew quickly as immigrants, mostly from Europe, came to make new lives.

In the South, cotton plantations kept things the same. As the plantation owners bought the best land for cotton, they pushed smaller farmers to land that was harder to farm. Some of these smaller farmers (including Abraham Lincoln's father) left the slave states and went to the free states in the Northwest Territory.

Chapter 4

Years of Compromise, 1819–1854

People in the North and the South did have one thing in common: They wanted more land. Farmers left the rocky soil of New England and went south and west to Pennsylvania. Soon pioneers were moving on to the Northwest Territory. As they moved west, the New Englanders took their way of life and their beliefs with them.

The cotton planters also looked west for better land. Cotton wore out the soil quickly, so the cotton planters went west to Kentucky, Alabama, and Mississippi.

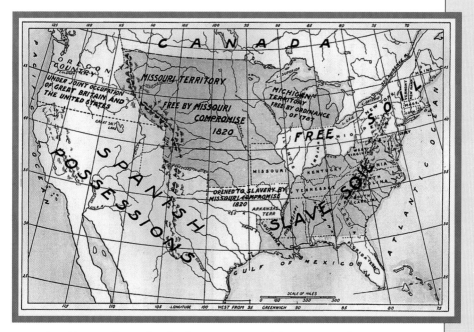

▲ This map shows the distribution in 1820 of free states and territories, where slavery was prohibited, and slave states, where it was allowed.

When President Jefferson bought the Louisiana Territory from France in 1803, the country suddenly doubled in size. Cotton planters wasted no time taking their slaves to Louisiana. Before long they went north to the Arkansas Territory and then on to Missouri. Northerners and Southerners alike talked about a country that would reach to the Pacific Ocean. The possibilities for more land seemed almost unlimited.

▶ A Delicate Balance

By 1819, nine new states had joined the original thirteen states. At that time there were eleven slave states (where slavery was legal) and eleven free states (where slavery had been abolished or had never been allowed). Although the states were evenly divided between slave and free states, the Southerners noticed a trend that worried them. The slave states were larger in area, but there were more people in the free Northern states. More people meant that Northern states had more votes in the House of Representatives. The Southerners wanted to be sure that at least half of the states would be slave states. The slave states might be a minority in the House of Representatives, but the Southerners were determined that they would not be a minority in the Senate.

The Southern planters worried about being a minority in the government because they were afraid of losing their slaves. The Constitution and the Fugitive Slave Act of 1793 required everyone in the free states to return any escaped slaves. Some Northerners did not like these laws, though, and did not obey them. Southerners worried that the Northerners could amend (or change) the Constitution and get rid of the part that said that escaped slaves had to be returned.

Statehood for Missouri

When Missouri requested statehood in 1819, Southerners rejoiced. Missouri already had ten thousand slaves and would join the Union as a slave state. Northerners were not as happy about it, though, because part of Missouri extended above the Mason-Dixon line. The Mason-Dixon line, named for the two surveyors who mapped it, marked the border between Pennsylvania and Maryland. Northerners had come to see the Mason-Dixon line as the border between free states and slave states, and they wanted the line extended into the west.

Suddenly, as Congress considered whether or not Missouri should become a state, Southerners thought their worst fears were coming true. A congressman from New York proposed that Missouri should gradually become a free state. His proposal passed the House of Representatives, where Northerners had a majority, but it did not pass in the Senate.

Henry Clay's ability to bring opposing sides together earned him the nickname the Great Compromiser. Clay was instrumental in getting Congress to adopt the Missouri Compromise, which forbid the expansion of slavery into territory lying above a certain line of latitude.

The Missouri Compromise

As Congress spent time debating the extension of slavery into the territories, Kentucky's Henry Clay, the Speaker of the House, convinced the House of Representatives and the Senate to accept a compromise that became known as the Missouri Compromise. According to the Missouri Compromise, Maine (which was still part of Massachusetts) would become a free state at the same time that Missouri became a slave state. The Missouri Compromise also said that, except for Missouri, slavery would not be allowed in the Louisiana Territory north of 36 degrees 30 minutes north latitude, which marked the southern border of Missouri.

The Missouri Compromise was important to the North and the South. Southern planters thought it protected their right to keep slaves in new states in the South. Northerners believed it would keep slavery in the South and away from their lives.

The Tariff of Abominations

The North and the South continued to grow in such different directions that the Civil War almost happened as early as 1833. The argument then was over a tariff, a tax on goods imported from another country.

While the South was selling to England and to the North, factories in the Northeast were making the same kinds of things that England was making, including cotton cloth. Northern factories competed with English factories for customers, but English products were often less expensive.

In 1816, Congress passed the first tariff to make English products more expensive. Southerners did not like the tariff because it meant that they had to pay more for many of the things they bought.

Twelve years later, Congress passed the Tariff of 1828, which greatly increased the existing tariff. Southerners referred to it as the Tariff of Abominations. The tariff was reduced in 1832, but it was not reduced enough to please Southerners.

Ordinance of Nullification

A leader in the Southern campaign against the tariff was the U.S. vice president at the time, John C. Calhoun from South Carolina. Calhoun eventually resigned that office to be elected to the Senate, where he could protest federal policies that he thought undermined the authority of the states. Resolutions passed in 1798 in Kentucky and Virginia had already asserted the sovereignty of states. Calhoun went further, though, arguing that a state had the right to decide whether a federal law was unconstitutional and unfair and did not apply in that state. In other words, a state could *nullify* a federal law. In November 1832, South Carolina passed an Ordinance of Nullification, which stated that the Tariff of 1832 did not apply in South Carolina.

U.S. President Andrew Jackson, left, and South Carolina senator John Calhoun, right, were key players in the battle over nullification in which South Carolina threatened to secede from the Union.

Andrew Jackson, the U.S. president at the time, was a Southerner and a slave owner who, like Calhoun, was also a firm believer in states' rights. The doctrine of states' rights is based on the Tenth Amendment to the U.S. Constitution. That amendment states that powers not explicitly given to the federal government by the Constitution are powers to be reserved by the states or individual citizens.

But Jackson also believed in the Union. He said that a state could not nullify a federal law, and that U.S. citizens owed their loyalty first to the country, then to their state.[1] President Jackson backed up his words with a threat to send fifty thousand troops to collect the tariff at the port of Charleston, South Carolina. In response, South Carolina's government called for ten thousand militiamen to prevent an invasion of federal troops.[2] When South Carolina threatened to secede, President Jackson said that a state could not leave the Union.

It looked, then, as if South Carolina and the United States might actually go to war. Calhoun did not really want war, and he quickly worked with Henry Clay, who had put together the Missouri Compromise, to develop another compromise. This compromise, the Tariff of 1833, gradually lowered tariffs over the next nine years.

South Carolina did not secede, and there was no war. But the conflict over what the federal government could tell a state to do was not resolved.

Abolitionists

About this time, several antislavery societies were formed in Boston and Philadelphia.[3] These antislavery people were called abolitionists because they wanted to abolish slavery. Within just a few years, people in Northern cities had formed more than five hundred antislavery societies. In 1835, abolitionists mailed more than one million notices and pamphlets about their beliefs—and some of them were mailed to the South.[4] The abolitionists were a small percent of the Northern population, but Southerners began to think that almost everyone in the North was an abolitionist.

By this time, no one in the South dared to speak against slavery. As long as cotton was king, slaves were needed on the plantations. Educating slaves or training them for any other kind of work was discouraged, and people stopped setting slaves free because it became illegal

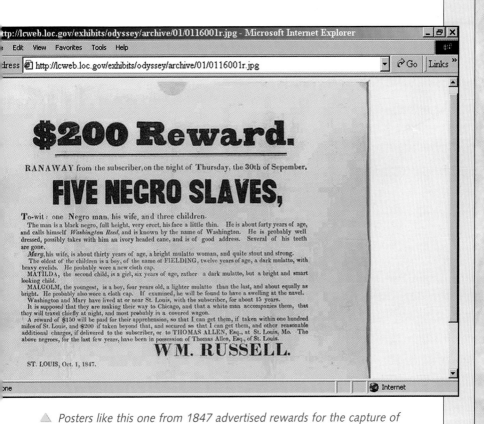

ttp://lcweb.loc.gov/exhibits/odyssey/archive/01/0116001r.jpg - Microsoft Internet Explorer

Edit   View   Favorites   Tools   Help

dress   http://lcweb.loc.gov/exhibits/odyssey/archive/01/0116001r.jpg   Go   Links

$200 Reward.

RANAWAY from the subscriber, on the night of Thursday, the 30th of September,

FIVE NEGRO SLAVES,

To-wit: one Negro man, his wife, and three children.

The man is a black negro, full height, very erect, his face a little thin. He is about forty years of age, and calls himself *Washington Reed*, and is known by the name of Washington. He is probably well dressed, possibly takes with him an ivory headed cane, and is of good address. Several of his teeth are gone.

Mary, his wife, is about thirty years of age, a bright mulatto woman, and quite stout and strong.

The oldest of the children is a boy, of the name of FIELDING, twelve years of age, a dark mulatto, with heavy eyelids. He probably wore a new cloth cap.

MATILDA, the second child, is a girl, six years of age, rather a dark mulatto, but a bright and smart looking child.

MALCOLM, the youngest, is a boy, four years old, a lighter mulatto than the last, and about equally as bright. He probably also wore a cloth cap. If examined, he will be found to have a swelling at the navel. Washington and Mary have lived at or near St. Louis, with the subscriber, for about 15 years.

It is supposed that they are making their way to Chicago, and that a white man accompanies them, that they will travel chiefly at night, and most probably in a covered wagon.

A reward of $150 will be paid for their apprehension, so that I can get them, if taken within one hundred miles of St. Louis, and $200 if taken beyond that, and secured so that I can get them, and other reasonable additional charges, if delivered to the subscriber, or to THOMAS ALLEN, Esq., at St. Louis, Mo. The above negroes, for the last few years, have been in possession of Thomas Allen, Esq., of St. Louis.

WM. RUSSELL.

ST. LOUIS, Oct. 1, 1847.

ne   Internet

Posters like this one from 1847 advertised rewards for the capture of African Americans who had escaped from slavery.

to do so. Some Southerners were convinced that slavery was good for the African Americans.

A Slave Rebels

Southerners feared that abolitionists would gain enough power in the government to end slavery, but there was something they feared more. At the same time that Southerners told themselves that slavery was good for African Americans, white people were afraid that abolitionists would encourage a slave rebellion. In 1831 a slave named Nat Turner did lead a small band of slaves in a rampage that left about sixty white people dead. Turner's rebellion was not the first, but it gained the most notoriety. In those days, before radio and television, rumors often traveled faster than news. Southerners heard rumors of hundreds of white people being killed before they ever got the real news, and they were frightened. In some parts of the South, there were many more black slaves than white people. A large slave rebellion would mean disaster for the white Southerners.

In 1835, Southern states passed laws to prevent people from talking about freeing the slaves. In fact, a Georgia law included the death penalty for anyone who published material that led to a slave rebellion.

The Compromise of 1850

Meanwhile the country continued to grow. In 1836, Texas won independence from Mexico. Then in 1848 the United States won the Mexican-American War, and suddenly the country had more than one million square miles of new territory. With the Treaty of Guadalupe Hidalgo, the United States was granted territory that would later become all or in part the states of Arizona, Utah, California, Nevada, New Mexico, Wyoming, and Colorado.

Southerners hoped to see more new slave states join the Union, but a Pennsylvania congressman named David Wilmot proposed that slavery should not be allowed in the new territory just as it was not allowed in the lands of the old Northwest Territory.

Southerners were angry. They had come to think that Congress did not have the right to tell any part of the Union that slavery would not be allowed. Southerners believed that, since slaves were property, the federal government should protect the slave owner's right to own slaves anywhere in the country.

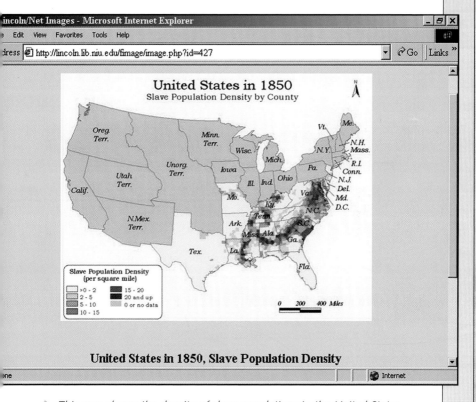

incoln/Net Images - Microsoft Internet Explorer

e   Edit   View   Favorites   Tools   Help

dress http://lincoln.lib.niu.edu/fimage/image.php?id=427   Go   Links

United States in 1850
Slave Population Density by County

Slave Population Density
(per square mile)

>0 - 2   15 - 20
2 - 5   20 and up
5 - 10   0 or no data
10 - 15

0   200   400 Miles

United States in 1850, Slave Population Density

ne   Internet

This map shows the density of slave populations in the United States in 1850.

The debates in Congress finally ended when, once again, Henry Clay put a compromise together. In 1850 that compromise became law.

To satisfy the Northerners, the Compromise of 1850 made California a free state and made it illegal to sell slaves in Washington, D.C. To make the Southerners happy, the compromise included a stronger Fugitive Slave Act and a promise that Congress would not interfere with slave trade between the states. The Compromise of 1850 also stated that the new territory east of California would be open to settlement by proslavery and antislavery settlers. The settlers themselves would then decide whether the territory would become a free state or a slave state. The idea that the people would decide for themselves was called popular sovereignty.

Thirty years earlier the Missouri Compromise allowed people in both slave and free states to feel safer. The Compromise of 1850 did not achieve the same result. For one thing, many Northerners hated the new Fugitive Slave Act. This law made it a federal crime to help an escaping slave in any way. For example, a person who gave food to an escaping slave could face a $1,000 fine and six months in prison. Even worse were the bounty hunters who captured free blacks, said they were runaway slaves, and took them south to be sold. Many Northerners saw the bounty hunters as kidnappers.

▶ Uncle Tom's Cabin

An abolitionist named Harriet Beecher Stowe hated the new Fugitive Slave Act so much that she wrote a book that was an attack on slavery. Although Stowe had never lived in the South, and she had known few slaves, she wrote about slaves trying to escape to freedom. That book was

Uncle Tom's Cabin. When the novel was published in 1852, people bought ten thousand copies in the first week.[5] Many who had never thought much about slavery felt sorry for the slaves in her story. It is said that when Abraham Lincoln met Mrs. Stowe later, during the war, he remarked, "So you're the little woman who wrote the book that started this great war."[6]

While abolitionists talked about freeing the slaves and Southern "fire-eaters" (those who most wanted the South to secede) talked about leaving the Union, most people in the United States thought about other things. Beginning in 1854, though, a chain of events sent ripples of fear and anger throughout the country.

A scene from Uncle Tom's Cabin, *left, and its author,* Harriet Beecher Stowe, *below.*

The End of Peace, 1854–1860

The trouble began because an influential senator from Illinois named Stephen A. Douglas had plans for the Nebraska Territory, which extended from what is now Oklahoma all the way to the Canadian border. Douglas was a supporter of manifest destiny—the belief that it was

Getting the Message Out Images - Microsoft Internet Explorer

File   Edit   View   Favorites   Tools   Help

Address http://lincoln.lib.niu.edu/fimage/dig/image.php?id=40

Done   Internet

▲ *Illinois senator Stephen A. Douglas was the leading proponent of popular sovereignty, which held that the residents of a territory had the right to choose whether or not to allow slavery there.*

the destiny of the United States to extend from the Atlantic Ocean to the Pacific Ocean. He also believed that the country needed railroads to connect the East and the West.

To help the country grow and to get the railroads he wanted, Douglas asked Congress to open the Nebraska Territory to settlers. This territory had already been promised to American Indians who had been driven from their homes in the East, but breaking that promise did not seem to be a problem for the congressmen. The problem was whether or not slavery would be allowed in the territory.

Southern congressmen looked at how much of the new territory lay north of the line of latitude that, according to the Missouri Compromise, marked the boundary of free territory. They did not want to see more free Northern states. Douglas needed their support to open the territory and get the railroads he wanted. He got their support by deciding that the Missouri Compromise should no longer apply to new territory.

The Kansas-Nebraska Act

Douglas rewrote the bill that would open the Nebraska Territory for settlement. According to his new bill, settlers would decide for themselves whether states formed from the new territory would be slave or free. Popular sovereignty had been accepted in the Compromise of 1850. Douglas thought it would work in the Nebraska Territory, too. His bill included the Southern position that Congress did not have the right to decide whether or not a territory could allow slavery. It made the Missouri Compromise null and void.

The new bill also divided the Nebraska Territory into two territories: Nebraska and Kansas. This division was

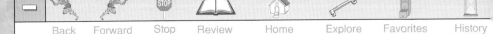
important to Southerners because the new Kansas Territory was more likely to become a slave state.

Southern leaders supported this bill, known as the Kansas-Nebraska Act, and Congress made it law. But Douglas and the Southern leaders "were astonished by the outrage that exploded across the North."[1] Northerners felt that the Missouri Compromise had protected them from slavery, and they were angry that Congress had passed a law that ended it. It seemed to Northerners that the government had given in to the South when it passed the Kansas-Nebraska Act, and they felt betrayed.

▶ "Bleeding Kansas"

Meanwhile, settlers from the North and the South rushed to make homes in the new territories. Northerners and Southerners who did not join the throng of settlers heading west took steps to influence what would happen in the territories. In New England, businessmen formed the Emigrant Aid Society, which helped about one thousand antislavery settlers get to Kansas.[2] A church in New York bought rifles for the antislavery settlers. People named these rifles "Beecher's Bibles" after the pastor of that church, Henry Ward Beecher, an abolitionist and the brother of

◀ Henry Ward Beecher, a brother of Harriet Beecher Stowe's, was a Congregational minister and abolitionist. Both he and his sister carried on their father's fight against slavery.

Harriet Beecher Stowe. When word reached the Southerners, they imagined armies of abolitionists armed with rifles. Southerners also helped settlers get to the new territory with their slaves. For eight years, Kansas became the scene of violent confrontations between antislavery and proslavery forces. These conflicts earned the territory the name "Bleeding Kansas."

In 1856 a band of Missourians called border ruffians terrorized the free town of Lawrence, Kansas. A man named John Brown took it upon himself to retaliate. His band of six men killed five proslavery men and two boys who had little or nothing to do with what happened in Lawrence. Far away in New England, abolitionists misunderstood what he had done and considered John Brown a hero.

Soon it was time for the people of Kansas to vote for a territorial legislature and become a state. Southerners could see that most Kansans would vote to make Kansas a free state, so about seventeen hundred Missourians crossed the border to vote illegally in the election. They helped elect a proslavery legislature, but the election was clearly a fraud. When antislavery Kansans held another election and elected an antislavery legislature, Kansas had two territorial legislatures.

President Buchanan chose to recognize the proslavery legislature, even though he knew it did not represent the people of Kansas. He put pressure on Congress to admit Kansas as a slave state.

The Dred Scott Decision

While Congress debated about Kansas, the Supreme Court put its weight solidly behind the South with its decision in the Dred Scott case. Dred Scott was the African-American slave of an army surgeon who took him from Missouri, a slave state, to army posts in the free Northwest. After his owner died, Scott brought his case to Missouri courts. His claim was that because he had lived in the free territories, he should be free. It took eleven years for the case to be decided finally by the Supreme Court, and Scott died nine months later. But the Supreme Court decision stirred people across the country.

The Supreme Court ruled that neither the Declaration of Independence nor the Constitution was ever meant to apply to slaves. In fact, according to the Supreme Court decision, even free African Americans were not entitled to the rights of citizens. The Supreme Court also ruled that the Missouri Compromise was unconstitutional because the federal government had no right to deprive citizens of property, including slave property. Until a territory became a state, the federal government was obliged to protect property owners.

Southerners were overjoyed, but Northerners were angry. First, Congress said the Missouri Compromise was null and void. Then the president supported a proslavery Kansas, even though the election was a fraud. Finally, the Supreme Court ruled that the federal government had no right to prohibit slavery in U.S. territories. Northerners

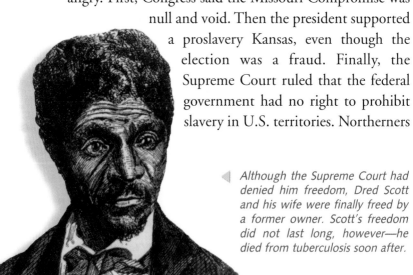

◁ Although the Supreme Court had denied him freedom, Dred Scott and his wife were finally freed by a former owner. Scott's freedom did not last long, however—he died from tuberculosis soon after.

felt that "Slave Power" ran the government even though the majority of people lived in the North. By 1860, about 18 million people lived in the free Northern states and only about 9 million people, including about 3 million slaves, lived in the slave states of the South.[3]

Southerners, on the other hand, were frightened by the number of antislavery settlers who surged into Kansas to vote against slavery in the new territories. They wanted Kansas to become a slave state. They were about to feel even more threatened.

John Brown

On October 16, 1859, John Brown and a band of about twenty white men and African-American men stormed the federal arsenal at Harpers Ferry, Virginia. Brown intended to lead slaves in a revolt throughout the South. His "army" was small, though, and slaves did not rush to support him as he had hoped. Two days after he seized part of the arsenal, Brown surrendered to federal troops. He was later tried and hanged.

For years, Southerners had been afraid that Northern abolitionists would begin a slave rebellion in the South. John Brown personified that

John Brown's stance against slavery went beyond that of other abolitionists. He believed that if slavery could not be ended by peaceful means, it would have to be ended with violent action.

fear. In fact, Brown was supported by many Northern abolitionists who saw him as a hero.

War on the Horizon

By 1860, when the political parties nominated candidates to run for the presidency, people were not in a frame of mind to think about compromise. There were four candidates: two from the South and two from the North. In the South, people tended to vote for John C. Breckinridge of Kentucky, a National Democrat, or John Bell of Tennessee, a Constitutional Union candidate. Northerners tended to vote for either Abraham Lincoln, a Republican, or Stephen Douglas, a Democrat.

Only one presidential candidate tried to reach the North and the South. Making use of the new trains, Douglas conducted the first nationwide campaign as he traveled from state to state and made speeches. Douglas

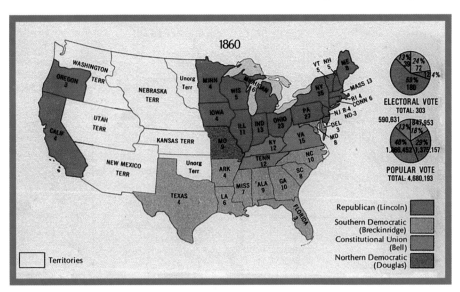

▲ This map shows the breakdown of free states, slaves states, and territories in the United States in 1860, the year that Abraham Lincoln was elected president for his first term.

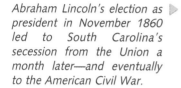

Abraham Lincoln's election as president in November 1860 led to South Carolina's secession from the Union a month later—and eventually to the American Civil War.

also told people that the country was in danger. He saw the Civil War coming, and he tried to warn people. Many Northerners could not believe that the South would really leave the Union. Many Southerners thought that they could leave the Union without a fight.

Lincoln received the most popular votes and the most electoral votes. In ten states in the South, though, not a single person voted for him. Still, people in one of those states celebrated when they heard the election results. Lincoln's election meant that South Carolina would secede from the Union.

From the very beginning of the country, the North and the South had compromised about arguments that involved states' rights, and the issue of slavery and the expansion of slavery into new territories was very much part of that argument. By 1860 it seemed that compromise was no longer possible. Southerners, with South Carolina taking the lead, believed that the federal government under Abraham Lincoln would undermine their sovereignty as a state and that their only choice was to leave the Union. The American Civil War could no longer be stalled.

Chapter Notes

Chapter 1. The Civil War Begins

1. Bruce Catton, *The Coming Fury* (Garden City, N.Y.: Doubleday & Company, 1961), p. 313.

2. Ibid.

3. Ibid., p. 303.

4. Ibid., p. 317.

5. Ibid., p. 324.

Chapter 2. North and South: Two Cultures, 1607–1790

1. Paul Johnson, *A History of the American People* (New York: HarperCollins Publishers, 1997), p. 9.

2. PBS, *Africans in America*, "Part 1: The Terrible Transformation, 1450–1750," n.d., <http://www.pbs.org/wgbh/aia/part1/map1.html> (June 27, 2003).

3. Johnson, p. 63.

4. Ibid., p. 74.

5. Kenneth Davis, *Don't Know Much About the Civil War* (New York: Avon Books, 1996), p. 10.

6. Johnson, p. 93.

7. Ibid., pp. 65–66.

8. Hugh Brogan, *The Longman History of the United States* (New York: William Morrow and Company, Inc., 1985), p. 96.

9. Davis, p. 8.

Chapter 3. Cotton, 1790–1818

1. Kenneth C. Davis, *Don't Know Much About the Civil War* (New York: Avon Books, 1996), p. 42.

2. Ibid., p. 43.

3. Ibid.

4. Paul Johnson, *A History of the American People* (New York: HarperCollins Publishers, 1997), p. 284.

Chapter 4. Years of Compromise, 1819–1854

1. Paul Johnson, *A History of the American People* (New York: HarperCollins Publishers, 1997), p. 347.

2. Kenneth C. Davis, *Don't Know Much About the Civil War* (New York: Avon Books, 1996), p. 60.

3. Ibid., p. 70.

4. Bernard Bailyn, David Bion Davis, David Herbert Donald, John L. Thomas, Robert H. Wiebe, and Gordon S. Wood, *The Great Republic* (Lexington, Mass.: D. C. Heath, 1977), p. 554.

5. Davis, p. 109.

6. Ibid., p. 110.

Chapter 5. The End of Peace, 1854–1860

1. Bernard Bailyn, David Bion Davis, David Herbert Donald, John L. Thomas, Robert H. Wiebe, and Gordon S. Wood, *The Great Republic* (Lexington, Mass.: D. C. Heath, 1977), p. 626.

2. Paul Johnson, *A History of the American People* (New York: HarperCollins Publishers, 1997), p. 428.

3. Peter J. Parish, *The American Civil War* (New York: Holmes & Meier, 1975), p. 21.

Further Reading

Bial, Raymond. *The Underground Railroad.* Boston: Houghton Mifflin Co., 1999.

Cinton, Catherine. *Scholastic Encyclopedia of the Civil War.* New York: Scholastic, Inc., 1999.

Collier, Christopher, and James Lincoln Collier. *Slavery and the Coming of the Civil War.* New York: Benchmark Books, 2000.

Fradin, Dennis Brindell. *Bound for the North Star: True Stories of Fugitive Slaves.* New York: Clarion Books, 2000.

Hakim, Joy. *A History of US, Book 5: Liberty for All.* New York: Oxford University Press Children's Books, 1999.

Isaacs, Sally Senzell. *America in the Time of Abraham Lincoln: The Story of Our Nation from Coast to Coast.* Chicago: Heinemann Library, 1999.

McCurdy, Michael, ed. *Escape From Slavery: The Boyhood of Frederick Douglass in His Own Words.* New York: Knopf, 1994.

Olson, Kay Melchisedech. *Africans in America, 1619–1865.* Mankato, Minn.: Capstone Press, 2002.

Peacock, Judith. *Secession: The Southern States Leave the Union.* Mankato, Minn.: Capstone Press, 2002.

Ray, Delia. *Nation Torn: The Story of How the Civil War Began.* East Rutherford, N.J.: Penguin Putnam Books for Young Readers, 1996.

Index